Giulio Gambarini

<u>PRAISE for the METHOD</u>

For entrepreneurs and managers that pursue
excellence and forget common sense.

*A small guide for those approaching accountable
positions within a company, and a heartfelt call back to
reality for those who already hold them.*

Praise for the Method

To
Rinaldo Carrel, Shlomo Doron, Biagio Lussi, Rolando Menendez, Luciano Micheli, Eliaz Poleg.
Friends and Mentors, in life and work.

Special thanks to my friend Alison Hunter, who has patiently helped me to review these pages.

English translation by Aurora Traduzioni – Rome
(Silvia Franceschetti – Valentina Angela Rattay)

Praise for the Method

Praise for the Method

Titolo | Praise for the Method
Autore | Giulio Gambarini

ISBN | 978-88-91178-11-4

© Tutti I diritti riservati all'Autore
Nessuna parte di questo libro può
essere riprodotta senza il
Preventive assenso dell'Autore.

Youcanprint Self-Publishing
Via Roma, 73 – 73039 Tricase (LE) – Italy
www.youcanprint.it
info@youcanprint.it
Facebook: facebook.com/youcanprint.it
Twitter: twitter.com/youcanprintit

Introduction

Dear reader,

For years, I have worked as a manager within companies in various countries, each different in size, structure, approach, culture, characteristics and goals. But yet, they all had an element in common, to which they were inevitably inclined: to get better results every year, compared to those of the year before. The impulse towards improvement is a wonderful and exciting goal that is, at the end, what distinguishes humans from the animals.

However, too often I have seen this wonderful ambition transformed into odd projects, becoming unrealistic and unattainable, or good projects carried out terribly, or simply too cumbersome to be sustained by a weak structure. Too often I have seen top-ranked managers planning excellent projects, but losing sight of the company's basic functions. Too often I have seen hasty and impulsive approaches to problems, without knowledge, logic or coherence, by getting to solutions that are revealed to be more detrimental than the problem itself.

No matter the structure, from the simplest to the most complex, every project is doomed to fail if it is not preceded by preparation, guaranteeing that the entire organization is aware of, and can implement, the blueprinted plan in a precise and controlled manner. And in order to get to this point, it is necessary to approach our work as managers in a way that, from the beginning, entails order, methodology, clear-sightedness and clear goals, for the sake of producing a corporate machine that precisely obeys our orders and that quickly communicates the warning signs of operations that do not work. The goal of this booklet is to help new managers to find a methodology and to learn to think about their actions before implementing them, as the Zen masters teach, and to help the most expert managers, who are probably overwhelmed with thousands of daily tasks, in remembering that order and moral discipline are necessary to get more with less stress. I hope that you may get interesting ideas and starting points for reflection, which, in particular, will help you to discover and regain pleasure and excitement in your work.

Happy reading,

Giulio Gambarini

Chapter 1
READY... GO!

The first day at a new company or in a new position:
You may enter from the lowest levels of the hierarchical scale, or from the highest ones, but the key suggestion that I want to give to everybody, in order to not get burned out from the beginning, to not create unwanted enemies and, respectively, to earn credibility, is to listen a lot, take note of everything and say little. The ideal thing to do in this situation is to think seven times about what you are going to say, and then...keep quiet! Instead, ask questions, examine in depth, when in doubt ask again. Almost all people love talking more than listening, so take advantage of this. Collect as much information as possible; take note of it and put it all together, so that you may form your own opinion and understand in detail how the organization works, what its weaknesses and strengths are, and how the dynamics of the processes function beyond what is found in the company's official documentation.
If you are at the lower levels of the hierarchical scale, then the organization will guide you

towards what they expect from you. However, your role will be more complex if you enter from the higher levels, since you will be only told about what does not work, and it will be up to you to understand a) what *truly* does not work, b) why it does not work, and c) how to change things so that it does work. When you are summoned to solve a problem, it's crucial to understand that the top management has already profiled a diagnosis and established the cure...without visiting the patient! It is astonishing how even at many companies today certainties are disseminated, causes are determined and solutions are based entirely upon emotions, without having the patience, the tools, or even the intellectual curiosity to get to the root of problems.

It may happen (not rarely, believe me) that a general manager has a foolish idea one day because that morning the production manager, who did not sleep well because of indigestion caused by the ratatouille consumed the evening before, responded hastily and superficially when they crossed paths in the hallway, thus causing a crack within the corporate structure. From that point on, any following episode is instrumental (often unconsciously) in widening this rift, until it becomes an abyss upon which an entirely inexistent world is constructed. And there's no one to blame but the ratatouille!

So you are called to bridge this abyss, and, maybe, you discover that the hole is not there at all, but somewhere else, unseen until now. Therefore, you not only have to take care of the problem, but also convince the person above you that attention has to paid to something other than what he had in mind, hoping that he will be intelligent enough to understand that he made a mistake and to accept a diagnosis different from his own without taking it as a personal offence.

I enjoy listening to everybody, on all levels. But during the first weeks at a company, I carry out a sort of suspension of judgement, wanting to form my own personal opinion, trying to hold valid the opinions that others would like to have me believe before I have the necessary elements to build my own - even if "the others" are higher up on the hierarchical scale.

The approach that I prefer when I have a new job is divided into three stages:

1. Interviews with colleagues and supervisors, to get a better idea about the company's general operations, its processes and its organization, and to get a rough idea about the persons that report to me.

2. A general meeting with my direct employees, all together, in order to explain who I am, why the company has hired me and upon which values I want to base my work with them. Take note: I talk about values and ethics, about approaches towards working life and being a team, not about solutions to problems that do not exist yet!

3. Individual meetings (which have to last at least a couple of hours each) with each person reporting directly to me, during which I seek to understand who he or she is, his professional (and often also personal) background, how his department has been organized, what contact and interaction he has with others, who the most reliable people are in his sector, what the major critical situations are and how he measures his performance.

After these first three steps, we still will not be perfectly knowledgeable about the entire company and all its dynamics (which may take years in order to be revealed in full detail), but we will certainly have a good general framework that at least will allow us to trace the guidelines that will be the base of our work.

You should doubt, a thousand times over, anyone who enters a company and already knows what to do without even having taken a moment for analysis and reflection. He probably has done this successfully somewhere else. However, that was a different place and time, and the same cure does not work equally on every patient. Or maybe not, maybe his way really is best way to intervene, but the importance of what's at stake requires at least some substantiation before taking the entire organization in a certain direction.

Learn to listen, to think, to collect data, to make objective analyses, to get acquainted with the dynamics and processes before formulating judgements. Solutions are to be found according to truly critical situations, not upon unverified voices that circulate around the company. Remember that each problem almost always has a solution that is easy, immediate and...wrong!

What would you say about a physician that prescribes you medication without any medical examination, based only on the description about your illness provided by your wife over the phone?

Chapter 2

THE TEAM: NEW, OLD, VINTAGE

Setting up a team of collaborators with whom we will manage our company is certainly the hardest challenge to face. This step has the highest number of restrictions that limit our movements, and also the highest number of fundamental, yet intangible, factors, all of which will influence the final result.

Companies usually already have established teams with which you must decide how to act. Unfortunately, managers still exist who are so superficial that, with fake, cowboy-inspired decision-making, they pursue a priori the fundamentalist theories of the kind "I want all new people, we have to shift gears" or, on the contrary, "we won't change anything, I want the company's continuity to be guaranteed".

It is not possible to build up a team without understanding what game is being played, without having studied the rules and without having clearly defined which goals we want to achieve and through which strategy.

A critical study of the organization and its current processes, examined through the lens of the objectives and strategies that we want to pursue, leads us to clarify what we should do differently, and to think of what type of company may be most functional in order to get where we want to be.

The result will be an organizational plan where each role doesn't yet have a person's name assigned to it, but the role's powers and responsibilities are defined in detail. When doing this kind of work, I enjoy (and have always enjoyed) thinking about the maxim "power without responsibility is useless, responsibility without power is idiotic". It helps to be both pragmatic and coherent.

The bureaucratic interpretation that too many Human Resource Departments give to job descriptions has significantly reduced their meaning to boring documents to fill out to complete an archive or in order to activate an external job selection. Instead they could (and should) be essential instruments for structuring the organization.

As a provocation, I can even understand that Human Resources may not have all job descriptions regarding the company's roles in its archive, but I do not approve of a manager lacking a clear and detailed definition for the roles of those that work in his team. Beware, I'm talking about roles, not people. I define the role, and the person assumes the role, not the other way around.

At the same time, along with the definition of the roles, we have to proceed with an evaluation of the people below the manager, analyzing those that are both the first and second levels below (sometimes one has also to climb down to the third). The evaluation can be carried out through various types of instruments (you can find a dozen scientific methods or pseudo-methods for staff evaluation online), or, hold on tight, through a primitive...face-to-face meeting!

Give people time to prepare themselves, so that they can present their education history, their story, their current work, their structure, their measurement methods and result evaluations, their ambitions and worries. Let them talk, listen to them and spend half an hour more, rather than half an hour less.

You will be astonished how this will shed light on the people and the company. But you have to do it in a structured manner, with the right timing, with an organized procedure that takes all the company's aspects into consideration. This enables you, on one hand, to gather knowledge about everything (or almost everything) that it is possible to formalize and measure. On the other hand, it will give you an idea about intangible factors, such as how much a person is accountable for in order to set up a change, how much this person is motivated and ambitious, what kind of relationship or problems he or she has with his or her colleagues, and - why not - what the levers and obstacles will be for working with this person. The half-completed conversations carried out in the hallway or while washing your hands are not only stupid, but even misleading: people are thinking about something else, they tell you the first thing that pops in their mind so that they can get rid of you quickly. Discussions carried out with only some members of the organization (and not with the entire group) are even more dangerous, since you will have a vision that is incomplete, unbalanced and...wrong! Therefore, please, no conclusions until you have completed the process; just take note and don't do anything else.

In the end, patiently putting the pieces together, you will sketch out the organization, with detailed and defined roles and a list of persons that you had the chance to get acquainted with, and you will ascertain that, with ease, you will be able to put them into the roles that you had defined earlier. Sometimes, because you are adaptable and not fundamentalists, you may even afford yourself the luxury of adapting the boundaries (not the basis) of some roles to suit the characteristics of a person: this isn't blasphemy!

The result, I'd wager, will be that your team will be made up of people that are a bit "old" staying where they currently are, some people from the second level that will take on responsibilities stemming from the first level, and some resources that you have to search for externally, maybe among your old acquaintances. However, you can only do this if you know exactly what you are searching for and only if you cannot find them internally, not for some stupid "clan" mentality, which is useless and harmful.

It would be wonderful to be able to set up a team worthy of esteem, in order to feel that you are a "primus inter pares", surrounded by co-workers with whom you may compare yourself with and mutually improve, even if your role entails the power (!) and the responsibility (!) to decide in which direction to steer the boat.

The de-structured definition of a team which is made of novices, who are often full of themselves, lacking methodology, and only guided by their current mood, has, very often, a typical way of revealing itself: the organization is split into pieces. Today this team announces a change, after two months another one, after three months a third one, which probably contradicts the first one, and with people that go from being lauded to losing it all in no time, and vice versa. The problem in such an organization is that, after a short time, everybody starts to defend himself, seeking to be exposed as little as possible, and the company does not take one step forward.

Setting up a team that survives in the course of time and that is productive is achieved through methods, patience, courage and vision. With pleasantries and momentary moods you invite, at most, people to a party; that hardly lasts longer than a few hours.

Chapter 3

I MEASURE, THEREFORE I AM

In every field of our existence where any type of "exchange" takes place, we always apply, more or less consciously, some sort of measurement. Even in relationships (friendship and love), in some way, we measure those that stand by our side, according to the extent a person makes us feel good or makes us laugh or how much he or she reassures us.

In the workplace, the ability to make these measurements is absolutely fundamental. It obliges us to clearly define the goals that we want to pursue, to decide which elements we want to implement in order to pursue them, to share goals and restrictions with the people working with us, and to check, frequently and mercilessly, if we are heading to the right direction. I have even seen strategies being modified because a serious evaluation of the key parameters showed that the seemingly logical and instinctive decisions made previously were totally unsustainable.

The first step is to define the KPI: the Key Performance Indicators. In contrast with what many managers think (who like to have lots of numbers, even if ultimately they are negligibly important and diminish focus instead of bringing benefits), the essential step lies with "K". We have to decide what the KEY indicators are, those that, if they are above the agreed values, are sufficient to certify that our company is solidly heading to the desired direction. The definition of the Key Indicators is a strategic choice, because it will lead the whole organization to primarily act in a way leading towards continuous improvement. Properly defining the indicators will also make it clear that, as a side effect of certain decisions made in pursuit of the key goals, negative trends regarding other indicators may occur (a common example is the choice between customer service and service at a stock level, even if this example is slightly out of date since new management models do not put the two parameters in competition with each other necessarily). We could then keep the first indicator as a key parameter, while also requiring that reaching this goal mustn't lead to another, secondary goal dropping under a certain level. A sort of restricted optimization exercise, if you like.

Do you understand the importance of the process I described above? It showed a goal to achieve, and it also showed the cost that it entails to reach it. In addition, I have shown that sometimes the cost is so high that the key goal has to be changed.

The definition of KPI involves the whole company, because it implies a necessarily in-depth knowledge about all its processes. If I do not know that a tyre contains air, I would never think of measuring its pressure; if I do not know that air enters and exits through a specific valve, I would never think of using that valve to measure the pressure. Detailed knowledge about the processes often belongs to the engineers rather than to the managers; for this reason, the KPI definition, and its subsequent accurate compilation, is the fruit of the entire organization's labour, involving different levels of the hierarchy. Here emerges the additional necessity to have neutral players (usually the Management Control area is employed for this), in order to certify that the survey method is consistent with the goals, and that the accurate compilation is carried out according to actual and incontestable grounds.

Once that the KPI are defined, it is clear that they will become the clearest, most objective way that is lacking in bad interpretations to communicate to the entire organization what results will be expected from everyone, and what boundaries they will have to respect. Beware, we are talking about results and boundaries, not about fondness or instinctive impressions: this means that if a manager delivers what we have asked from him, he is doing a good job and that's that. It does not matter if we like this person or not. If, despite the achieved results, we decide anyway that the manager is not right for our company, this means that we have poorly defined goals. We have to remember that these goals do not have to necessarily be about costs or consignments or sales, they may also be less tangible aspects (I have seen companies successfully measure safety politics or the coherence of ethical values between the organization and its managers).

True professionals want and appreciate this sort of quantitative approach, with the KPI. However, those that grew up in companies where relationships, friendship, and nepotism represented the bedrock for professional growth tend to slip away from actual measurements, both blocking the definition of their indicators and making a thousand exceptions to their interpretation.

It is important to note that the interpretation of indicators must show improvement over time, applying significant time values (usually monthly or quarterly intervals), and the trend, rather than absolute values, is what should be measured. It is indeed rather thorny to make evaluations of the KPI by comparing different companies. Often, the basis of these indicators and their included outer limits are so inconsistent that a comparison of different companies is impossible or, worse, completely misleading.

The KPI are necessary, obviously, not only to measure the others, but also, especially, to see clearly if the choices we have made are rewarding the company or not. In the face of the rest of the world we can invent all possibly conceivable excuses, but inside our closed office, in front of numbers that are heading in the wrong direction, we have to ask ourselves honestly if there is something to improve in our decisions.

The supermen, the enlightened, those that are above everything, rarely define clear and unambiguous KPI that make it possible to measure the quality of the work carried out without any sort of discussion about it. A serious indicator is also a measurement of how well they are able to carry out their work: it does not lie; it does not bend to the will of limitless egos. It talks and that's it; it does not accept denial. And this does not at all please those who are used to cohorts of bootlickers willing to tell you how great and intelligent you are.

The KPI are the sextants and compasses of our ship, they enable us to understand where we are and to decide where to steer to in order to get to our destination. Would you board a ship where the captain does not know how to use the sextant and has lost the compass?

Chapter 4

FLAPSI HAPSI, or about Time Management

Time, if you think hard about it, is probably the only resource that is completely external to our lives. Since we do not talk about quantum physics, but about everyday normal life within the conditions that we can sense on our small planet, we have to accept that there is no way to extend time or make it run faster, not even if you are the richest and most powerful person on earth. Depending on what you do and on who you are, it may seem that it runs faster or that it is slowing down, but in reality it always runs at the same speed.

In our professional life, we may decide to extend our working hours in order to get more done, but at the price of sacrificing all the other things we could do in that time, such as dedicating ourselves to our families or to our hobbies or, simply, resting. It's a high price, in any case, which has to be weighed carefully before being paid. What do I mean by that? Well, simply that before extending our work hours, we should be sure that we are already spending our working hours as efficiently as possible. Then, if this is the case, we may possibly extend our workday, but not without having done an appropriate analysis about our working organization. I do not even want to take into consideration the cases where you have to stay longer at work because you have a boss who is a bit bewildering and who judges anyone who leaves work earlier than eight p.m. to be shirking their duties. If that is the case, there may be no other alternative than to let him read this booklet! Let's get back to us and to our time management. First of all, let's be sure to understand the concepts: our daily activities are divided into moments to see people (appointments) and other moments (sometimes overlapping with the first ones) during which you have to do something (activities).

The planning of my day will be, therefore, a sequence of appointments, and between one interval and the other, I will have to integrate my activities, that is, the things that have to be done. It is clear that we are talking about a puzzle: if a day is crammed full of appointments, one after another, my activities (or at least those that I do not want to carry out during the appointments) must necessarily be very limited, simply because I don't have the time to carry them out.

The other way round is also true: if during a certain day I have to carry out consuming activities that eat up a lot of time, I must limit the number of appointments. The time container has a limited capacity, and beyond a certain limit, if I add something, I must remove something else.

Do not start with excuses like "this is a nice theory but the real world is completely different". This is absolutely not true, and only by trying, will you see how a well-organized approach can lower stress in addition to increasing your efficiency, and thus doing the same work in less time.

But in order to succeed, an instrument is necessary: an agenda, which nowadays, in my opinion, should be electronic and linked to the e-mail account. Leaving aside the banal aspect that an agenda contains addresses and telephone numbers, an electronic agenda enables you to efficiently organize appointments (which get added to your calendar when you are invited to and accept a meeting) and activities (where you can add the date on which they have to be carried out). Therefore, for instance, looking at your agenda for the following week (or a day, month, or year), you will find a figurative representation, with immediate impact, about the appointments scheduled and, for each day, the activities that you have planned to carry out. You will see immediately if what you have planned is workable or if you need to change something, perhaps even anticipating some of the activities you had planned to carry out to a later time. Indeed, it is possible that you find out that you have half a day empty, which you now must use in order to balance the following days, which are desperately overcrowded, or to do the things, at last, that you are have postponed.

The agenda on the computer, by the way, also has two more essential advantages:

1. Being linked to the e-mail account, you can look at it not only in your office, but also directly on your smart phone or tablet wherever you are;
2. It enables you to save, directly in the appointment or activity entry, notes, annotations, links, and memos, and to share them with whomever you want.

Good, now it is clear that days are made of appointments and activities, and you have an instrument to handle them. But this is not enough to guarantee efficiency, you still have to manage, at the same time, other two essential elements: inconveniences and periodicity. An inconvenience certainly is an unforeseen mishap (and for this you have to think up something in the moment it happens and plan your agenda differently - unfortunately there is no other way). But is also represented by that colleague (*Flapsi Hapsi*, in the definition formed by TMI in the last century) that knocks at your door and asks "do you have 5 minutes?" If you give him those "5 minutes", you are dead, goodbye to planning and goodbye to efficiency. You have to learn that the answer is NO, you don't have 5 minutes. In order to ask questions or to share their concerns, people have to make an appointment and plan when to meet up (and possibly also what to prepare before the meeting). It is not about getting formal or bureaucratic, it's about efficiency, and about the company's money that is burned by those that do not understand this simple concept, who may also be the CEO or the managing director.

By periodicity I mean a deterrent to inconveniences, because – as I have seen first hand - timely appointments with colleagues or employees at regular, fixed intervals, means that people tend to bring their doubts and requests to these fixed appointments and no longer ask for those "5 minutes", scattered during the worst moments of the week. The only exception is for *real* emergencies that, by this point, truly are filtered down to the minimum. I used to spend one hour a week, every week, face to face with those directly reporting to me. Every week or every two weeks, I had other appointments with almost everyone else, and I have to say that this kind of approach always worked quite well.

The nice thing about this method, which we discussed in the preceding pages, is that your agenda will be made of encounters, things to do, notes about what you have done, and everything stays well structured within a calendar, moment after moment. In the evening, before you leave the office, it is enough to glance at the things that you will have to do in the days to come, or shift some of the scheduled activities or appointments if you believe that they are not well planned, and then go. You can go home without concerns, aware of what will await you and sure that it is organized in the best way possible, without keeping anything in mind, since the computer will do it in your place.

When I think about the fact that there are still people that go to their offices and invent their daily schedule all of a sudden, I feel bad for them. You will see them get lost in the most inconclusive things for days and then work absurdly during the night or during weekends without any rest when a deadline approaches, acting like great heroes that are willing to make big sacrifices for their work. Sacrifices that are in many cases (not in all cases, for heaven's sake, maybe there are some exceptions) self-inflicted and useless, and are not of any use to the company.

Time may be master or servant, it is up to us if we want to be dominated or we want to dominate it, by means of the mentioned method, discipline and intelligence.

Chapter 5

TO DECIDE OR NOT TO DECIDE?

Life is a series of continuous decisions, one after the other, second after second: stay in bed or get up, grab a book with our right or left hand, spend our evening at the pub or at the cinema, study sculpture or engineering, put the family or work first, retire as soon as possible or at the latest possible time, get healthcare for a bad disease or to die. Decisions, all decisions: some are irrelevant and others essential, some seemingly irrelevant but in reality essential, and vice versa. We cannot escape this necessity while in the office, at work; we have to make decisions continuously. These decisions will have consequences that primarily affect our company's results, but also our quality of life, our relationship with our colleagues and, last but not least, the judgements that others make about us.

And here we get to the first fundamental point for a correct and efficient decision-making process: we have to understand, clearly and objectively, the consequences (direct and indirect ones, in the short and long run) of the decisions we have to make. Deciding what colour should be the folder in which you put the documents regarding production is not the same thing as deciding the layout of a production facility. Obvious…? Actually it is not always, not for everybody. One of the most serious problems that I have identified among some of my managers has been their difficulty in determining a scale of importance and priorities in the decisions they had to make, with the result that they dedicated more or less the same amount of attention to different things. This does not work, it cannot work: the negligible decisions may, actually have to be, taken quickly, without remarkable in-depth analysis and time wasted. They would take away resources from important decisions, which deserve attention, verification and countercheck levels instead, in an almost obsessive way. An error in the choice of the folder probably does not have any consequences, or anyway, if it has any, they will be unimportant and remediable. An error in determining the layout of a production facility is a catastrophe for the company. The problem is that, while the difference between the folder and the layout is obvious, it is not obvious for the other infinite decisions that lie in between, with the risk of taking important decisions lightly and analysing negligible decisions in-depth and for days.

It is not possible to skip establishing a range of importance; it is an exercise that has to be done every time, and we must have the potential consequences of the decision clearly in mind in order to *decide* how to handle it.

Then, less banal than it seems, we have to ask ourselves what are the alternatives, the possible paths that we may take. Often, you will be asked to choose between two alternatives, yet whomever has presented them to you has not thought of the fact that there may be a third and a fourth option. The good manager comes to light in this situation: he does not stop in front of the obvious path, but he explores other possibilities as well, and has the strength to give them up if he finds out that they are actually unfeasible. In doing so, he also helps co-workers make decisions. Sometimes one is presented with matters that do not necessitate real decisions, but only a confirmation of clear solutions: confirm, but also make sure that the employee realizes that he or she came asking for a support in taking actions, not for a decision.

You may also consciously choose to postpone a decision - if you believe that you do not have enough information, for example - because it is not the right time to decide. There is nothing wrong with this, but keep in mind that deciding not to decide is also a decision, and it will definitely have consequences.

Complex decisions have a series of resulting factors to take into consideration, which tend, unfortunately, to move disharmoniously. For example, deciding to buy a low-cost item saves you money, but it also often means (but not always) you get a low-quality product. Therefore, what to do, how to decide? There is no secret formula, you have to make it up on your own: it helps me to list all factors (cost, sturdiness, suitability for the task, customer support, etc.) and to give to each a weight: the heavier it is, the more important it is. Then, I list all the options and I give each one a grade for each factor. I multiply the grade by the weight and I sum everything up: the options with the highest votes are usually the most interesting ones. Of course, take what I said with a grain of salt, this is not an unquestionable science, it is a simple arithmetic transposition of subjective evaluations, but it helps at least to create order where many parameters are at stake. No extremism: the final score is not compulsory, it is just a practical system in order to get oriented within complexity.

However, when you make a decision, be a man until the end, take on full fatherhood for it, for better and for worse, weigh its effects (do you remember the aforementioned KPI?) and evaluate the consequences honestly, at least to yourself.

What you will decide to sell or to present to others is your business, it depends on your professionalism and conscience, your values and the environment in which you work: but you have to put yourself in a position to know, at least a priori, if a decision made in a precise moment has been right or wrong, otherwise you cannot learn, and therefore cannot improve.

The manager is the person that makes decisions, and based upon those decisions, the company experiences success or failure. A good manager keeps calm, approaches problems methodologically and therefore makes the best decisions in the hardest moments, and is not scared in front of complex dilemmas with potential consequences. Those that are not able, due to culture, mentality, or character, to make decisions and to take the full responsibility for them, cannot be in charge of managerial offices.

Chapter 6

It's easier SAID than DONE...

There's the rub! Whoever is gifted with the slightest intelligence (or just with the gift of gab) is able to say what should be done and maybe also how, but only a few, very few, have the moral strength, method, perseverance, and awareness to transform general statements about intents into practical facts.

Let's learn to be suspicious of verbs that are conjugated without spelling out who the subject is: *"it would be necessary to"*, *"it has to be done"*, *"there is the need to"*. These words do not clearly identify who has to do something; is a useless chatter that ends in itself, only good to swell the chest of some irrelevant turkey of irrelevant.

But, be aware of one thing: I talk about moral strength because taking care of a project's implementation leads to an inevitable and obvious taking charge of responsibility. In the end, either things work out (and it is your merit) or they do not work out (and it is your fault), *tertium non datur* [ie, a third solution is not available — translator's note]. Those that are afraid to expose themselves, those that prefer to stay hidden in the darkness, those that aim at calm survival instead of the adrenalin rush originating from the set up of something practical, should stay away from the execution of a project. Too dangerous, too visible, too measurable.

In addition, the execution a project needs an organized and precise approach that anticipates hurdles and enables the most efficient solution possible. It is a preparatory and inevitable step that has to be developed well by the company's Board, regarding the well-structured definition of the goals, boundaries and obligations of the project.

Starting from here, an orchestra has to be built up where, in front of a common and shared arrangement, everybody plays his own instrument with virtue and passion. Without venturing into daring organizational constructions, we aim to set up a Project Team according to clear roles.

I like this kind of structure:

1. **Sponsor** (nominated by the Board, he or she should be a volunteering member of the Board): he is a senior manager at the company, motivated practically so that the project leads to objective results within the allotted time. He is the intermediary between the Project Team and the Upper Management; this is the person who makes sure that the whole hierarchy proceeds actively when a hurdle

appears on the path that requires the intervention of higher-ups for its removal.

2. **Leader** (nominated by the Board): he or she is the head of the project, the person that feels the project is "his own". He chooses the Team, motivates, directs, and guides it in drafting and implementing the plan of action, activates the Sponsor when there is a hurdle, calls and leads the Team meetings, he bears the honour and burden of updating, for better or worse, the company's Board about the project's development. The Leader has the duty, before setting up the Team, of comparing his view with that of the Sponsor and Board in order to be sure to have a very clear understanding about the goals, the boundaries and the obligations of the Project.

3. **Team Members** (nominated by the Leader): select team members according to their competencies and powers (direct or representative ones), so that they perform the company's functions that will mainly influence the project and/or will have an impact. I do not like Teams that

are too big, let's try to stay within teams with no more than 5 or 6 members; there is nothing that prevents us to invite *ad hoc* guests whenever we face situations that are not covered by the regular team members.

Once the team is set up, the first fundamental step (after sharing the Project with all team members) is the drafting of an Action Plan: a series of actions, indicating who will carry them out and their deadlines, which will lead step by step to the Project's completion. An Action Plan, even if it has to be considered a commitment towards the Board, it is not the bible written in stone - it can and has to be adapted to different situations that will emerge as work proceeds. Some unforeseen steps will be added, some will be removed, and others will be simply scheduled differently; an Action Plan that changes many times but considered by the team at every moment as a practical working device, is preferable. On the other hand, an Action Plan that remains unchanged over the course of time risks turning into a pure academic exercise, that progressively loses any practical value. The Action Plan is a guiding reference point at each Team's meeting (I suggest that the meeting should take place at least every two weeks, longer intervals loosen the tension towards the goal), the starting-tool to see what has actually been achieved, and to share the next steps to carry out. If it is well done, with clear data about the activities that have been completed on time, those that are delayed but will not have any effect on the project's delivery time, and those that are delayed but that undermine the schedule and the success (use colours, green/yellow/red, they have an immediate impact), it may also be a tool through which the Sponsors and the Board may be kept up-to-date about the work status, thus diminishing the frequency of meetings of the Management Committee (which do often steal time for the preparation of presentations that do not have much to do with the project's success).

Even so, we always also include moments of formal verification and validation from the Board in the Action Plan, during which we will ask the Upper Management to confirm their commitment and will to proceed with the project, in light of costs and organizational observations, in addition to the path they want to take when faced with alternatives that could lead to considerably different Project results.

An essential comment: this kind of approach has to be applied not only to far-reaching strategic projects, but also to every project that you want to convert from a statement of purpose into an actual fact. The sponsor may be a department head, the leader a shift supervisor and some of the team members workers, the project may be less formal and less structured, but the concept does not change: everything should be simpler, slimmer, more immediate, but never improvised, never left to chance or to the uncontrolled good will of an individual.

Each project requires planning, preparation and structure; otherwise it will remain in the heads of those who conceived it without ever becoming reality.

The "make it happen" concept is a job for true, experienced, disciplined professionals, that are hardliners, that do not have time for small-talk because they are too busy to turn their dreams into reality.

Chapter 7

THE UTOPIA OF OMNIPRESENCE: MOTIVATION, DELEGATION, CONTROL

I once read a beautiful sentence, that for me best explains what motivation is: "a company is made of three kinds of capital: invested capital, circulating capital, human capital. The last kind of capital has a specific particularity that distinguishes it from the other two: on every evening it leaves the company, and you have to give it a good reason to come back the next day". We, as managers, have to try to understand which levers guide the people working with us, in order to incite their ambition to improve, and to avoid setting off certain negative reactions that could lead a person to work in unproductive conditions. We all know that the possibility to get a bonus, a career advancement, or a company benefit can, in most cases, lead to virtuous turns.

However, we often forget that there are other elements that may nullify those positive powers, and lead people to work poorly, unproductively, or even in a direction that is opposite to the one the company desires. And here we're talking about cornerstone elements of human existence, in whatever field: the need to be acknowledged, knowing that somebody is listening to our opinion and that it is taken into consideration, feeling like an integral part of a project and a team, having influence on the final result, experimenting with new methods without a firing squad ready to execute us in case of a mistake, being sure that the company will not dump us like an old shoe if we should be going through a rough patch. These were all concepts that became common in culture in the 80's and 90's, and that were blown away with the arrival of the crisis. Companies know that there are fewer job offers than job seekers, and therefore have the rational confidence that their employees won't leave, since they have few other available alternatives. From this stems, more or less declared, the winding return to the conviction that people have to be thankful to have a job and a salary, and that, therefore, they shouldn't bother the manager too much with their whims. A pertinent Dilbert cartoon says that human resources dropped to the ninth position of companies' priorities since copy paper is in the eighth position.

Go ahead like this, cowboy entrepreneurs and managers who think to build a future upon machismo and mistreatment (and it is not a question of gender, also some women play the same role, without distinction). You will be successful in levelling everybody to the ground and in demonstrating to yourself that you were right to treat everybody to a kick in their rear, since nobody was able to bring new ideas or results. Because even if it is in the mid term rather than in the short term, capable professionals can always find an alternative, right? Those that stay put, even in the long run, and accept behaviours that insult their dignity and professionalism are weak and timid - unable to resell themselves, they never expose themselves and do not bring anything new to the table because their only true goal is to keep their job. And so begins the first loop of a downward spiral, that will lead you and your companies to hit the ground and, then, to go down further.

It will seem like you cannot trust anybody and, therefore, that you cannot delegate anything. He who delegates assumes that the person who receives it has:

1. A good reason to accept the mandate
2. Clear purposes to pursue and clear boundaries to respect
3. A clear definition of the boundaries regarding decision making and powers he has
4. The ability to make reasonable decisions

5. A reasonable certainty that the decisions taken will not be contradicted and nor distorted by people above him/her
6. Objective instruments that make it possible for anybody, on whatever level, to consistently measure the consequences of his decisions

These six points depend predominantly on the people higher up in the hierarchical scale - on those that delegate! Also, point 4, the one regarding decision-making, in the end depends on the boss, who has also the task of choosing people that are able to make reasonable decisions. Delegating is always necessary, in different degrees according to the complexity of the company, but it always exists. In a big company, the President will delegate the head of the Operations to choose the suppliers, therefore making decisions that will have consequences of tens, if not hundreds, of millions of Euros. In a micro-company made up of the owner and a secretary, where the latter has the task of answering the phone and talking to those contacting the company, we are in front of a delegation, which must be studied and managed accordingly, and not left to chance as often happens.

Sometimes there are delegation processes that seem to be a passing of the buck, which is typical within areas that are considered less strategic for the company (but not necessarily just there). In these cases, delegating is meant as "I do not want to know about these things, therefore take them up and do not bother me". Good, nothing to say about that, but there has to be, in any case, some way to check on the progress being made. It is clear that testing strategic areas will allow us to have a daily view about the evolution of what we have delegated, while within less strategic areas we may afford forms of verification that have longer intervals (I would never wait longer than a month); however, we need to put in place something that tells us how things are going. Otherwise, we will face surprises - always bad ones - when we least expect them: we will be annoyed by the fact that the person we have delegated has proven to be incompetent and dumb. Actually, I am sorry, we are the incompetent and dumb ones, since we turned the engine of our car on, engaged first gear, put the foot down and forgot to steer and look where we were going.

Also remember that well organized, managed and controlled delegation is also necessary to guarantee a better quality of life (we do not have to assist others in all decisions and at all times, enabling us to work less and to concentrate on the issues that are truly important) and it gives us the possibility to present ourselves for positions of greater wider responsibility within the organization. At higher levels, delegation is a necessity, not just a choice, and it is better to learn how to handle it well, from the beginning. Those that do not know how to delegate are operative people and cannot be called managers; they have to work exclusively alone, otherwise they will make mistakes.

Motivation is the engine that moves every person, making somebody decide how many of his talents he wants to use in his field, in exercising his specific task. Then, through delegation, these talents are put into a condition that can be expressed. But, in the end, the circle has to be closed by an adequate testing system, necessary to fine-tune the engine and to steer properly.

Chapter 8

IT TAKES ALL KINDS TO MAKE A WORLD: EVALUATIONS

During the course of our working life (and not only), we have to interact with people that are very different in terms of culture, education, walks of life, origin, character and habits. This fact is beautiful in itself, but only if we are able to interpret these differences as a reason for moral and cultural enrichment, and if we do not try to dictate to the entire universe the behaviour and the attitude that, according to our own criteria, are the only acceptable ones.

There are boundaries according to which all behaviours have to be directed (for instance, we cannot permit anybody to have discriminatory or violent behaviours, there is no acceptable reason for it), but within these boundaries we have to be sure that everybody feels free to express him/herself according to his or her personality, competencies, and values.

A manager's main job is to make sure that everyone brings the highest possible value to the company, according to their characteristics. This does not mean that all employees have to adjust to a behavioural prototype that is reassuring for the ego of the hierarchical boss. This does not at all mean leaving the organization to anarchy, but rather deeply understanding the personality of each person and finding the right way to permit everybody to assert their strengths as much as possible and to limit the effects of their weaknesses as much as possible.

There are very good managers that have shy, introverted personalities, others that are equally good and empathetic, yet extroverted. We may see excellent results achieved by risk-adverse managers with an essentially technical education, equal to what is achieved by managers that are braver and more creative. Within the same position, doing the same job, there is no effective cookie-cutter professional profile that can be compared to a "wrong" one. In the end, only intelligence and the ability to adapt count, the rest is only small talk for those that are mentally too lazy to call some easy stereotypes into question. But the growth of our co-workers, the fact that they have the ability to give their best does not, once more, depend on coincidences, but rather on our ability to help them by giving advice and through the timely responses that we give to their behaviour. We mustn't fear that these co-workers may grow to an extent that could endanger our position: if there are very capable employees this will happen anyway, it does not matter how much you play the defence.

However, also keep in mind your being replaceable may potentially mean in a positive way: that a co-worker that is prepared and trained in order to take the responsibility of your position. This may make you more vulnerable because you are less essential, but you may also be nominated for more interesting positions when the right occasion presents itself.

I am convinced that the failure of a co-worker is also a failure for us. Evidently, we have not been able to find, together with the co-worker, a productive way to use his qualities. Unless you choose, consciously, to dismiss him in order to let someone else take his position or in order to give different signals to the organization. This is a choice, a cynical one if you like, but it is still a choice; in other cases it is a failure, on multiple levels, useless to beat about the bush.

Besides the steady management of people (I did not write it at random, I really mean *people*, a word that encloses a boundary that is much wider than the depreciative word *managers*) through regular one-on-one meetings and the regular sharing of objectives and achieved results (the KPI's, once again), I always found so-called "appraisals" to be useful, when done biannually or annually.

An appraisal is an individual meeting between the boss and the employee, that lasts at least a couple of hours, during which impressions and comments about mutual behaviours are shared, weak and strong areas that have been highlighted during the last months are discussed, formative plans are prepared in order to help the employee improve the areas in which he is most deficient, middle term goals are set, and the achieved results are discussed.

This is not a trial; there is no judge that passes judgements with regard to an accused person. It is an exchange of ideas, the occasion during which it is possible to solve some misunderstandings or to acknowledge mutual merits. The appraisal does not help the personnel department in order to make the archive heavier, it helps you and your employee do even better, touching upon performance and also relational aspects.

In order to have an organized and focused discussion, there are structural models to follow, that usually concern managerial, functional, potential competencies and ambitions, goals that have been achieved and that have to be achieved, and training to apply in the field.

At the next appointment, after six months or one year, you start again from the previous appraisal, evaluating the development achieved towards the set goal.

Try it out, if it is well done (with the right preparatory considerations, honesty and sensitivity) I guarantee this will also help to reinforce the human relationship between the boss and the co-worker, with all the advantages that result from it.

Everyone has his own characteristics; it is the boss' difficult and exciting job to find a way to use them as best as he can. Maybe it is impossible to change people, but it is possible, and one has to succeed in it, to soften the edges that make us particularly sharp and that are not suitable for a job within a team.

Chapter 9

THE REAR-VIEW MIRROR

Almost all companies that can be proud of existing for at least a medium amount of time (let's say longer than 10/15 years), may also be proud of at least one great success: unfortunately.
I have put two provocative adverbs, one at the beginning and one at the end of the sentence.
The word "almost" at the beginning indicates those companies that are successful in developing and achieving incredible results, even if they are poorly managed, one management after the other. Classically, those are overvalued companies, due to speculative "bubbles" of the moment (the new economy at the end of the nineties is an evident example), in which certain conditions, especially those regarding emotions and moods, lead investors to gamble that the changes that are taking place in that moment will transform something that has been a donkey all along, into a racing horse. But I am not really interested in these companies, I can only envy those that take advantage (usually great advantage and usually beyond any personal merit of their own) from these situations, and I can only be happy not be in the shoes of those that get ruined from these situations. However, I am

interested instead in the other kind of company, the one that can be "unfortunately" proud of at least one great success. I repeat: I hope it is clear that the word "unfortunately" is only a provocation. I wish all companies only moments of great success, because without success no company can continue to exist, of course.

But success, if on one hand it enables the creation of resources that permit the company to continue to exist and to develop, on the other hand it has to be handled with extreme care. Success blinds us; it makes us believe that we discovered a magic formula, in which what worked well at a certain point in time will work well forever.

There are many companies that were established in the 60's and 70's, experiencing a steady development until the first half of the 90's, and which, from that point on, have started to experience a progressive decline or even a fall, that caused their heavy reshaping if not, directly, their closure. And many of these companies have spent the last disastrous 20 years trying to rebuild the same identical conditions which brought them to success 40 years ago, blaming a too-shy sales manager or a designer who is not creative enough for the repeated failures that are entirely due to lack of strategy and organization.

Wake up! The huge transformation of the market in the middle of the 90's is cultural on every level; it does not only concern the internet, globalization and distribution. The huge transformation also involved the transition from business relationships (consisting of professional relationships shuffled with personal relationships, involving suppliers, customers, co-workers, employees, etc.) to business optimization (in which it is necessary to pursue the best option, regarding every aspect, that there might be in a precise point in time).

I do not want to say that we should hop, merely upon opportunistic bases, from one option to another without suitably taking into consideration how important a certain level of stability is in order to guarantee a good operation of all processes. But it is obvious that when discussing an important contract renewal, we shouldn't be limited to the three representatives that are in front of us, but we must widen our survey to everything that is available, possibly, everywhere in the world. If the spokesperson in front of us ends up being the best option (or at least, one of the best ones, since proximity may be a parameter to add to the evaluation of the offer) we will sign the contract with him, otherwise we will make an agreement with somebody else.

In a world that has changed in this way, so radically, there are still some crazy nostalgic people (and there are more than you think) that pursue the reconstruction of something that cannot exist anymore, convinced that by bringing the endogenous variables back to the last success, will lead also the company automatically to the last achieved success. Pretend that Ferrari at the Formula One World Championship 2014 shows up with the car that won the price in 1979, and you will get an idea about their odds of winning…

Those are the companies where you try to introduce change and you get as a reply "ah, we did that in 1987 and it didn't work", those for whom a core competency involves knowing the industry that they work in, having already dealt with problems that may show up in the future. You may recognize these companies at first glance by the fact that employees are immensely proud to be part of the company, and according to them, all other companies in the sector are nothing compared to the one they work for. This is the first symptom of the fact that they probably will not be inclined to search for new paths because, if they have not taken that course before, it probably is wrong. The fact that they do not speak Spanish or know how to deal with a Vietnamese supplier becomes negligible; they feel self-important just by being part of a certain company. And the drama is that there are still some Managing Directors who believe in this self-reference and that set their company up based upon this.

Trying not to be extremists, I believe that we can get a good example from the United States: baseball is a sport that has been nourished all along by statistics in order to evaluate the performance of players. In order to select new talents, one had to address to expert observers that went around the fields of the whole country, in order to select those that showed a good potential. For some time now, the statistical data is combined (built upon the career of the players, that can be equated to the talent under consideration, such as the average score, physical structure, family environment, studies, etc.) with the traditional, in-person observations, in order to produce a more reliable chart about a potential growth. The modern observer therefore has to combine technical/psychological skills with the ability to use statistical tools; by now, an expert old-style observer who follows only his intuition has proven to be much less effective than an average level observer that *also* has a good mastery of statistical tools.

Therefore there is room not only for experience (which definitely counts, don't get me wrong), but also, and especially, for those that have the ability to catch the signs of transformation, for those that know how to interpret them, for those that invent new ways of doing things, being perfectly aware of the fact that the context in which we are living is not and cannot be the as it was years ago.

Those that lead a company have to be focused on the path before them; their attention has to be entirely there.

The road we have taken has taught us how our car behaves in certain occasions, and a glance to the rear-view mirror enables us to understand if, in respect to our progress, there are some dangers that may lay it on the line. All this is valuable and important, but not so much to make us forget to look ahead.

Our survival depends on the way we face the bends that we have to deal with, not on how we faced the ones that are behind us. Would you head down a mountain road at 130 kilometres per hour just because the first half of your journey was on a highway, where you were able to speed ahead without any danger?

Chapter 10

THE DARKENED ILLUMINATION

It has been recently discovered that brain cells can be regenerated. Before, it was believed that we had an initial "endowment" at birth, and that those cells were it for a lifetime, even after progressive losses.

For us, theoretically, this doesn't change much: in either case, our brain at any given moment is not exactly the same as it was earlier. If we had a stroke of genius in 1972, it is likely that those three brain cells that lead us to this stroke of genius have left us long ago.

Thus, just because you had an extraordinary idea at a certain point in your life doesn't mean that your ideas from that point on will be extraordinary as well. Some may be extraordinary, some other ideas will be just so-so, and still others inevitably will be a load of bollocks. I am not saying that an intelligent person may become a total idiot, but I believe that we should aim for a healthy balance and an honest evaluation of ourselves, both after great failures, and, even more difficult, after great successes.

I am not a great soccer expert and I think that interviews with football players and trainers are extremely banal. Sportswriters ask certain questions that are not of any interest to anybody, and the interviewee has to choose between: a) I played well (victory), b) it was the referee's fault (defeat), c) I like it here (contract renewal, and then he leaves anyway, after two months). But Josè Mourinho, who at the time was Chelsea's coach, really thrilled me one night. The reporter, expecting that Mourinho would enjoy prattling on in self-celebration after an important victory (as 99% of his colleagues would have done), asked him: "Coach, you substituted X with Y, and Y scored! Then you substituted W with Z, and Z scored! What would you call this?" And Mourinho, in return, replied literally: "Stroke of good fucking luck!" Exactly. Good fucking luck, translated less vulgarly, luck. You need a bit of luck to get anywhere, but you do not get anywhere if there is not even a hint of luck. A fortuitous encounter opens some doors to us, a specific moment where our ideas are the key that the world was waiting for, the loss of a job that forces us to reinvent different means. At the right moment.

Then, if we put these two things together - that is, a) having a brilliant idea once does not mean that all our ideas are brilliant, and b) the success we have achieved is also somewhat the result of luck - maybe we can avoid falling into the trap of a Eulogy to Ourselves. This is made evident in expecting the company you are leading to flatten itself before the Cult of Personality of those that have had at least one great success story, where the cornerstone positions are assigned to those that show the right amount of admiration for the boss, where those that challenge, question things, and do not fall in line are considered corrupt individuals that have to be eradicated. But, development comes precisely from diversity, from non-conformism, from freethinking, from the right to criticize. A boss does not fill his role in order to satisfy his need for reward; his job, his task, his responsibility, his duty, is to select the most brilliant minds and to put them in a position to bring about to the best possible results for the company.

When we see companies where the hierarchy is full of people that come from distant mutual acquaintances, from subaltern relationships consolidated over the course of time, by blood relationships of various kinds, we have to suspect that the person who leads the company wants to keep his authority without putting it into play daily, that he is in a comfortable position where he commands in virtue of what he has been able to do in the past. And, therefore, he believes he is a guardian of the Truth, the only person able to reach the most appropriate conclusions, and nothing should tarnish the pseudo-godly veil that he has draped himself with.

Actually, everyone (even the most enlightened ones) has a moment in which he is exhausted, unable to suggest a change in pace, where he does not come up with the right idea at the right time. And a person cannot have the obtuse presumption of considering himself enlightened if he does not have any awareness of his limits.

A truly smart person, really confident, really enlightened, will surround himself with brilliant minds that help him to overcome the moments in which his mind is clouded and his creativity is blocked.

An idiot will surround himself with yes-men, drawn around him like a monument against which everybody, the boss included, will slam into sooner or later, and what's worse, bringing the company along with them.

Companies are terrifyingly full of these idiots.

But there are some key phrases that enable us to flush them out, to unmask them with certainty. Sometimes, these sentences are not said clearly and explicitly, but the actions of these individuals make us understand that they think as follows:

1. "I have identified in branch X the problem that is stopping the company from getting

off the ground, therefore I must go and take up the matter personally". Don't you have anything else to do? Can't you control a branch based on performance indicators? Can't you motivate a co-worker, based on clear, critical factors for success? Or, on the other hand, have you no idea about what is going on and are you only guessing randomly, hoping that your presence alone will instil godly light to that entire sector?

2. "I have a team that follows me everywhere, they've been with me for a long time, I trust them blindly". Aren't you capable of selecting new managers? Are you afraid about a young person that may overshadow you? Don't you know how to measure performances and do you realize that anybody could fool you without your noticing it?

3. "Anybody that does not align to my point of view has to leave". Why might somebody not agree with your point of view? Because, maybe, you do not have one? Because you are not able to explain it? Because it is so weak that, even if you

explained it, nobody would consider it valid? And, regarding what has been said above, do you really think that those that do not align to your point of view, will be so idiotic (like you) to tell you?

Essentially, to keep it short: I do not know if God exists. But I know for sure that if he exists, he does not dedicate himself to leading companies.

Chapter 11

THE CRISIS

"Let's not pretend that things will change if we keep doing the same things. A crisis can be a real blessing to any person, to any nation. For all crises bring progress. Creativity is born from anguish, just like the day is born from the dark night. It's in crisis that inventiveness is born, as well as discoveries made and big strategies. He who overcomes crisis, overcomes himself, without getting overcome.
He who blames his failure to a crisis neglects his own talent and is more interested in problems than solutions. Incompetence is the true crisis. The greatest inconvenience of people and nations is the laziness with which they attempt to find the solutions to their problems. There's no challenge without a crisis. Without challenges, life becomes a routine, a slow agony. There's no merit without crisis. It's in the crisis where we can show the very best in us. Without a crisis, any wind becomes a tender touch. To speak about a crisis is to promote it. Not to speak about it is to exalt conformism. Let us work hard instead. Let us stop, once and for all, the menacing crisis that represents the tragedy of not being willing to overcome it."

Albert Einstein

I take Einstein's statement as valid, but let's be honest: if this wasn't written by a great genius, but the name of a third-rate politician instead (choose the name, I don't think that you will have any problem thinking of one), we would feel entitled to tell him to get lost and to set these pearls of wisdom immediately aside, into the banality basket.

Don't get me wrong, Einstein isn't entirely wrong. Crises can lead us to think about ourselves, about how we set up our existence, to invent a new path and, maybe, to find better ways to live personally and professionally. During crises, the best ones emerge - this is true. But it is also true that those who are not the "best" die. And if we are always ready to tell ourselves about this or that individual who, because of the crisis, has reached levels that were previously unimaginable, rarely do we hear about those that, during the hard times of a crisis, unfortunately, give in.

A friend of mine, years ago, got a bad disease. The physician, giving him his diagnosis, said: "anyway, I can't say that this will be a walk in the park, but there is an 80% chance of recovery from a disease like yours. I hope that this will reassure you". My friend, during a moment of cynicism also during the worst times, replied: "doctor, I will get be reassured if you can tell me that I will not be among the 20% that does not heal". And, indeed, he died.

The real issue is exactly this: we try to take advantage of a crisis (or crises) in order to progress, to change, to get better; we make a virtue of necessity. But nobody searches voluntarily for a crisis, because we know that some will stay in the field, and it could be us. Because we are not always sure (not in every situation, not in all points in time) that we are among the best. Maybe we have been among them in the past, maybe we will be again in the future, but nobody knows if we will among them in the exact moment where a crisis arises.

And then, certainly, we'll fight, we won't be crushed by the crisis; let's invent other ways to live and to work, everything is acceptable! But, if it is possible, we avoid crises, we try to avoid external factors obliging us to change and we struggle not to make mistakes that a crisis may bring.

Being ready to face adversity and knowing how to bear a downpour does not mean avoiding work and acting so that these adversities and these downpours don't even have a chance to happen.

SUMMARY

In this booklet we dealt with companies and with working life in general, this is the boundary we decided to stick to. For sure, a company is a microcosm in which personal dynamics are an approximation of what happens in private life. For sure, what we are at work is what we are at home as well. Nobody, if unless desperately schizophrenic, has such a dual personality that he is able to be only Dr. Jekyll on one side and only Mr. Hyde on the other. In reality, one of the two roles prevails according to the situation we are in. Of course, we spend a good part of our lives at work – it's not negligible. Well, then, ok: if, starting from company matters told by a boring engineer, you have learned something good that may be useful in other fields of your existence, then I will not object. In fact, I might even be happy about it, since it is, perhaps, the only reason that I wrote this book.

Buen Camino.

www.ingramcontent.com/pod-product-compliance
Lightning Source LLC
Chambersburg PA
CBHW051351150726
48000CB00003B/1137